LION OF THE HEART

Called 'Jelaluddin Balkhi' by the Persians and Afghans, Rumi was born on September 30, 1207, in Balkh, Afghanistan, then a part of the Persian Empire. Between 1215 and 1220, he and his family fled the threat of the invading Mongols and emigrated to Konya, Turkey; it was sometime after this that he became known as 'Rumi' meaning 'from Roman Anatolia'. His father, Bahauddin Walad, was a theologian and a mystic, and after his death Rumi took over the role of sheikh in the dervish learning community in Konya. Rumi pursued the life of an orthodox religious scholar until 1244 when he encountered the wandering dervish, Shams of Tabriz. After an exchange of religious ideas Shams and Rumi became inseparable friends, transported into a world of pure, mystical, conversation. This intense relationship left Rumi's students feeling neglected, and, feeling the ill-will, Shams disappeared. After news of Shams came from Damascus, Rumi's son was sent to bring him back, and the mystical conversation, or *sohbet*, began again. After Shams' second disappearance (he was probably murdered), and a period spent searching for his lost friend, Rumi came to the conclusion that Shams was now a part of him. Further concluding that when he wrote poetry it was Shams writing through him, he called his huge collection of odes and quatrains *The Works of Shams of Tabriz*. Following Shams' death Rumi had two other mystical companions, firstly Saladin Zarkub, a goldsmith, and then, after Saladin's death, Husam Chelebi, Rumi's scribe and student. It was Husam that Rumi declared the source of his vast six-volume masterwork *Mathnawi*. After twelve years of work on this masterpiece Rumi died on December 17, 1273.

Coleman Barks is Emeritus Professor of English at the University of Georgia in Athens, Georgia. Since 1984 he has, in collaboration with various Persian scholars, worked on translations of Rumi's poetry. Many consider that this compendium set, originally published as *The Essential Rumi*, has made the 13th-century mystic the most read poet in the United States.

Lion of the Heart

RUMI

Translated by COLEMAN BARKS
with JOHN MOYNE
A. J. ARBERRY
REYNOLD NICHOLSON

ARKANA
PENGUIN BOOKS

ARKANA

Published by the Penguin Group
27 Wrights Lane, London w8 5TZ, England
Penguin Putnam Inc., 375 Hudson Street, New York, New York 10014, USA
Penguin Books Australia Ltd, Ringwood, Victoria, Australia
Penguin Books Canada Ltd, 10 Alcorn Avenue, Toronto, Ontario, Canada M4V 3B2
Penguin Books (NZ) Ltd, 182–190 Wairau Road, Auckland 10, New Zealand

Penguin Books Ltd, Registered Offices: Harmondsworth, Middlesex, England

These translations first published in the USA in *The Essential Rumi* by HarperCollins 1995
Published by Arkana 1998
10 9 8 7 6 5 4 3 2 1

Set in 10/12.5 pt PostScript Monotype Bembo
Typeset by Rowland Phototypesetting Ltd, Bury St Edmunds, Suffolk
Made and printed in Great Britain by Clays Ltd, St Ives plc

*for the compassionate heart within the mind, the light within the body,
for the sun, Shams of Tabriz*

Contents

On Rumi

Persians and Afghanis call Rumi 'Jelaluddin Balkhi'. He was born September 30, 1207, in Balkh, Afghanistan, which was then part of the Persian empire. The name *Rumi* means 'from Roman Anatolia.' He was not known by that name, of course, until after his family, fleeing the threat of the invading Mongol armies, emigrated to Konya, Turkey, sometime between 1215 and 1220. His father, Bahauddin Walad, was a theologian and jurist and a mystic of uncertain lineage. Bahauddin Walad's *Maarif*, a collection of notes, diarylike remarks, sermons, and strange accounts of visionary experiences, has shocked most of the conventional scholars who have tried to understand them. He shows a startlingly sensual freedom in stating his union with God. Rumi was instructed in his father's secret inner life by a former student of his father, Burhanuddin Mahaqqiq. Burhan and Rumi also studied Sanai and Attar. At his father's death Rumi took over the position of sheikh in the dervish learning community in Konya. His life seems to have been a fairly normal one for a religious scholar – teaching, meditating, helping the poor – until in the late fall of 1244 when he met a stranger who put a question to him. That stranger was the wandering dervish, Shams of Tabriz, who had traveled throughout the Middle East searching and praying for someone who could 'endure my company.' A voice came, 'What will you give in return?' 'My head!' 'The one you seek is Jelaluddin of Konya.'

The question Shams spoke made the learned professor faint to the ground. We cannot be entirely certain of the question, but according to the most reliable account Shams asked who was greater, Muhammad or Bestami, for Bestami had said, 'How great is my glory,' whereas Muhammad had acknowledged in his prayer to God, 'We do not know You as we should.'

Rumi heard the depth out of which the question came and fell to the ground. He was finally able to answer that Muhammad was greater, because Bestami had taken one gulp of the divine and stopped there, whereas for Muhammad the way was always unfolding. There are various versions of this encounter, but whatever the facts, Shams and Rumi became inseparable. Their Friendship is one of the mysteries. They spent months together without any human needs, transported into a region of pure conversation. This ecstatic connection caused difficulties in the religious community. Rumi's students felt neglected. Sensing the trouble, Shams disappeared as suddenly as he had appeared. Annemarie Schimmel, a scholar immersed for forty years in the works of Rumi, thinks that it was at this first disappearance that Rumi began the transformation into a mystical artist. 'He turned into a poet, began to listen to music, and sang, whirling around, hour after hour.'

Word came that Shams was in Damascus. Rumi sent his son, Sultan Velad, to Syria to bring his Friend back to Konya. When Rumi and Shams met for the second time, they fell at each other's feet, so that 'no one knew who was lover and who the beloved.' Shams stayed in Rumi's home and was married to a young girl who had been brought up in the family. Again the long mystical conversation (*sohbet*) began, and again the jealousies grew.

On the night of December 5, 1248, as Rumi and Shams were talking, Shams was called to the back door. He went out, never to be seen again. Most likely, he was murdered with the connivance of Rumi's son, Allaedin; if so, Shams indeed gave his head for the privilege of mystical Friendship.

The mystery of the Friend's absence covered Rumi's world. He himself went out searching for Shams and journeyed again to Damascus. It was there that he realized,

Why should I seek? I am the same as
he. His essence speaks through me.
I have been looking for myself!

The union became complete. There was full *fana*, annihilation in the Friend. Shams was writing the poems. Rumi called the huge collection of his odes and quatrains *The Works of Shams of Tabriz*.

After Shams's death and Rumi's merging with him, another companion was found, Saladin Zarkub, the goldsmith. Saladin became the Friend to whom Rumi addressed his poems, not so fiercly as to Shams, but with quiet tenderness. When Saladin died, Husam Chelebi, Rumi's scribe and favorite student, assumed this role. Rumi claimed that Husam was the source, the one who understood the vast, secret order of the *Mathnawi*, that great work that shifts so fantastically from theory to folklore to jokes to ecstatic poetry. For the last twelve years of his life, Rumi dictated the six volumes of this masterwork to Husam. He died on December 17, 1273.

A Note on the Organization

The design of this series of Rumi books is meant to confuse scholars who would divide Rumi's poetry into the accepted categories: the quatrains (*rubaiyat*) and odes (*ghazals*) of the *Divan*, the six books of the *Mathnawi*, the discourses, the letters, and the almost unknown *Six Sermons*. The mind wants categories, but Rumi's creativity was a continuous fountaining from beyond forms and the mind, or as the sufis say, from a mind within the mind, the *qalb*, which is a great compassionate generosity.

The nine divisions here and the twenty-seven in the series are faint and playful palimpsests spread over Rumi's imagination. Poems easily splash over, slide from one overlay to another. The theme of these nine sections might be said to be the work required on the path of the dervish, the fierce pickaxe attention and the submission to a daily practice. The unity behind, *La'illaha il'Allahu* ('there's no reality but God; there is only God'), is the one substance the other subheadings float within at various depths. If one actually selected an 'essential' Rumi, it would be the *zikr*, the remembering that everything is God. Likewise, the titles of the poems are whimsical. Rumi's individual poems in Persian have no titles. His collection of quatrains and odes is called *The Works of Shams of Tabriz (Divani Shamsi Tabriz)*. The six books of poetry he dictated to his scribe, Husam Chelebi, are simply titled *Spiritual Couplets (Mathnawi)*, or sometimes he refers to them as *The Book of Husam*. The wonderfully goofy title of the discourses, *In It What's in It (Fihi Ma Fihi)*, may mean 'what's in the *Mathnawi* is in this too,' or it may be the kind of hands-thrown-up gesture it sounds like.

All of which makes the point that these poems are not monumental in the Western sense of memorializing moments; they are not discrete entities but a fluid, continuously self-revising, self-interrupting *medium*. They are not so much *about* anything as spoken from *within* something. Call it enlightenment, ecstatic love, spirit, soul, truth, the ocean of *ilm* (divine luminous wisdom), or the covenant of *alast* (the original agreement with God). Names do not matter. Some resonance of ocean resides in everyone. Rumi's poetry can be felt as a salt breeze from that, traveling inland.

These poems were created, not in packets and batches of art, but as part of a constant, practical, and mysterious discourse Rumi was having with a dervish learning community. The focus changed from stern to ecstatic, from everyday to esoteric, as the needs of the group arose. Poetry and music and movement were parts of that communal and secretly individual work of opening hearts and exploring the mystery of union with the divine. The form of this collection means to honor the variety and simultaneity of that mystical union.

Most of the facts, dates, and chew-toys for the intellect are stashed in the Notes.

Rumi puts a prose prayer at the beginning of each book of the *Mathnawi*. Here's the blessing he gives before Book IV.

Praise to Early-Waking Grievers

In the name of God the Most Merciful, and the Most Compassionate.

This is the fourth journey toward home, toward where the great advantages are waiting for us. Reading it, mystics will feel very happy, as a meadow feels when it hears thunder, the good news of rain coming, as tired eyes look forward to sleeping. Joy for the spirit, health for the body. In here is what genuine devotion wants, refreshment, sweet fruit ripe enough for the pickiest picker, medicine, detailed directions on how to get to the Friend. All praise to God. Here is the way to renew connection with your soul, and rest from difficulties. The study of this book will be painful to those who feel separate from God. It will make the others grateful. In the hold of this ship is a cargo not found in the attractiveness of young women. Here is a reward for lovers of God. A full moon and an inheritance you thought you had lost are now returned to you. More hope for the hopeful, lucky finds for foragers, wonderful things thought of to do. Anticipation after depression, expanding after contraction. The sun comes out, and that light is what we give, in this book, to our spiritual descendants. Our gratitude to God holds them to us, and brings more besides. As the Andalusian poet, Adi al-Riga, says,

I was sleeping, and being comforted
by a cool breeze, when suddenly a gray dove
from a thicket sang and sobbed with longing,
and reminded me of my own passion.

I had been away from my own soul so long,
so late-sleeping, but that dove's crying
woke me and made me cry. *Praise*
to all early-waking grievers!

Some go first, and others come long afterward. God blesses both and all in the
line, and replaces what has been consumed, and provides for those who work
the soil of helpfulness, and blesses Muhammad and Jesus and every other
messenger and prophet. Amen, and may the Lord of all created beings bless
you.

1. The Pickaxe:

Getting to the Treasure Beneath the Foundation

ON THE PICKAXE

One view of identity is that it's a structure made of what we *identify* with. Rumi says that identity must be torn down, completely demolished along with its little tailoring shop, the patch-sewing of eating and drinking consolations. Inner work is not all ecstatic surrender. Don't listen too often, Rumi advises, to the comforting part of the self that gives you what you want. Pray instead for a tough instructor. Nothing less than the radical disassembling of what we've wanted and gotten, and what we still wish for, allows us to discover the value of true being that lies underneath. The *pickaxe*, for Rumi, represents whatever does this fierce attention-work: clear discernment, a teacher's presence, simple strength, and honesty with oneself. The pickaxe dismantles the illusory personality and finds two glints in the dirt. Like eyes they are, but these jewel lights are not personal. Rumi points to a treasure within our lives unconnected to experience. It is intrinsic, beyond calculation, a given, reached after the ego is cleared away and a one-pointedness digs under the premises.

Who Makes These Changes?

Who makes these changes?
I shoot an arrow right.
It lands left.
I ride after a deer and find myself

chased by a hog.
I plot to get what I want
and end up in prison.

I dig pits to trap others
and fall in.

I should be suspicious
of what I want.

Why Wine is Forbidden

When the Prophet's ray of intelligence
struck the dim-witted man he was with,
the man got very happy, and talkative.

Soon, he began unmannerly raving.
This is the problem with a selflessness
that comes quickly,

                as with wine.

If the wine drinker
has a deep gentleness in him,
he will show that,

                when drunk.
But if he has hidden anger and arrogance,
those appear,

                and since most people do,
wine is forbidden to everyone.

On Resurrection Day

On Resurrection Day your body testifies against you.
Your hand says, 'I stole money.'
Your lips, 'I said meanness.'
Your feet, 'I went where I shouldn't.'
Your genitals, 'Me too.'

They will make your praying sound hypocritical.
Let the body's doings speak openly now,
without your saying a word,
as a student's walking behind a teacher
says, 'This one knows more clearly
than I the way.'

The Dream That Must Be Interpreted

This place is a dream.
Only a sleeper considers it real.

Then death comes like dawn,
and you wake up laughing
at what you thought was your grief.

But there's a difference with *this* dream.
Everything cruel and unconscious
done in the illusion of the present world,
all that does not fade away at the death-waking.

It stays,
and it must be *interpreted*.

All the mean laughing,
all the quick, sexual wanting,
those torn coats of Joseph,
they change into powerful wolves
that you must face.

The retaliation that sometimes comes now,
the swift, payback hit,
is just a boy's game
to what the other will be.

You know about circumcision here.
It's full castration there!

And this groggy time we live,
this is what it's like:
                          A man goes to sleep in the town
where he has always lived, and he dreams he's living
in another town.
                          In the dream, he doesn't remember
the town he's sleeping in his bed in. He believes
the reality of the dream town.

The world is that kind of sleep.

The dust of many crumbled cities
settles over us like a forgetful doze,
but we are older than those cities.
                                    We began
as a mineral. We emerged into plant life
and into the animal state, and then into being human,
and always we have forgotten our former states,
except in early spring when we slightly recall
being green again.
                    That's how a young person turns
toward a teacher. That's how a baby leans

toward the breast, without knowing the secret
of its desire, yet turning instinctively.

Humankind is being led along an evolving course,
through this migration of intelligences,
and though we seem to be sleeping,
there is an inner wakefulness
that directs the dream,

and that will eventually startle us back
to the truth of who we are.

The Pickaxe

Some commentary on *I was a hidden treasure,*
and I desired to be known: tear down

this house. A hundred thousand new houses
can be built from the transparent yellow carnelian

buried beneath it, and the only way to get to that
is to do the work of demolishing and then

digging under the foundations. With that value
in hand all the new construction will be done

without effort. And anyway, sooner or later this house
will fall on its own. The jewel treasure will be

uncovered, but it won't be yours then. The buried
wealth is your pay for doing the demolition,

the pick and shovel work. If you wait and just
let it happen, you'll bite your hand and say,

'I didn't do as I knew I should have.' This
is a rented house. You don't own the deed.

You have a lease, and you've set up a little shop,
where you barely make a living sewing patches

on torn clothing. Yet only a few feet underneath
are two veins, pure red and bright gold carnelian.

Quick! Take the pickaxe and pry the foundation.
You've got to quit this seamstress work.

What does the patch-sewing *mean*, you ask. Eating
and drinking. The heavy cloak of the body

is always getting torn. You patch it with food,
and other restless ego-satisfactions. Rip up

one board from the shop floor and look into
the basement. You'll see two glints in the dirt.

Zikr

A naked man jumps in the river, hornets swarming
above him. The water is the *zikr*, remembering,
There is no reality but God. There is only God.

The hornets are his sexual remembering, this woman,
that woman. Or if a woman, this man, that.
The head comes up. They sting.

Breathe water. Become river head to foot.
Hornets leave you alone then. Even if you're far
from the river, they pay no attention.

No one looks for stars when the sun's out.
A person blended into God does not disappear. He, or she,
is just completely soaked in God's qualities.
Do you need a quote from the Qur'an?

All shall be brought into our Presence.

Join those travelers. The lamps we burn go out,
some quickly. Some last till daybreak.
Some are dim, some intense, all fed with fuel.

If a light goes out in one house, that doesn't affect
the next house. This is the story of the animal soul,
not the divine soul. The sun shines on every house.
When it goes down, all houses get dark.

Light is the image of your teacher. Your enemies
love the dark. A spider weaves a web over a light,
out of himself, or herself, makes a veil.

Don't try to control a wild horse by grabbing its leg.
Take hold the neck. Use a bridle. Be sensible.
Then ride! There is a need for self-denial.

Don't be contemptuous of old obediences. They help.

The Core of Masculinity

The core of masculinity does not derive
from being male,
nor friendliness from those who console.

Your old grandmother says, 'Maybe you shouldn't
go to school. You look a little pale.'

Run when you hear that.
A father's stern slaps are better.

Your bodily soul wants comforting.
The severe father wants spiritual clarity.

He scolds but eventually
leads you into the open.

Pray for a tough instructor
to hear and act and stay within you.

We have been busy accumulating solace.
Make us afraid of how we were.

*   *   *   *

I honor those who try
to rid themselves of any lying,
who empty the self
and have only clear being there.

*   *   *   *

Dervish at the Door

A dervish knocked at a house
to ask for a piece of dry bread,
or moist, it didn't matter.

'This is not a bakery,' said the owner.

'Might you have a bit of gristle then?'

'Does this look like a butchershop?'

'A little flour?'

'Do you hear a grinding stone?'

'Some water?'

'This is not a well.'

Whatever the dervish asked for,
the man made some tired joke
and refused to give him anything.

Finally the dervish ran in the house,
lifted his robe, and squatted
as though to take a shit.

'Hey, hey!'

'Quiet, you sad man. A deserted place
is a fine spot to relieve oneself,
and since there's no living thing here,
or means of living, it needs fertilizing.'

The dervish began his own list
of questions and answers.

'What kind of bird are you? Not a falcon,
trained for the royal hand. Not a peacock,
painted with everyone's eyes. Not a parrot,
that talks for sugar cubes. Not a nightingale,
that sings like someone in love.

Not a hoopoe bringing messages to Solomon,
or a stork that builds on a cliffside.

What exactly do you do?
You are no known species.

You haggle and make jokes
to keep what you own for yourself.

You have forgotten the One
who doesn't care about ownership,
who doesn't try to turn a profit
from every human exchange.'

2. Art as Flirtation with Surrender:
Wanting New Silk Harp Strings

ON FLIRTATION

The design on the curtains is *not* what they conceal. Artists love shapes for enclosure, the chained cup beside the waterfall as a way of tasting the waterfall and maybe even the presence of someone meditating in the cave behind it. Forms keep splitting their chrysali, but the old harper wants *one* more set of silk strings. Some sufis have seen the beauties of art as something that can slow down soul growth. Art gives a teasing taste of surrender without the full experience. Beautiful poetry can keep one on the verge of the oceanic annihilation in God. Rumi says, we've been walking in the surf holding our robes up, when we should be diving naked under, and deeper under.

Omar and the Old Poet

The harper had grown old. His voice was choked sounding
and harsh, and some of his harp strings were broken.

He went to the graveyard at Medina and wept. 'Lord,
you've always accepted counterfeit coins from me!
Take these prayers again, and give me enough
to buy new silk strings for my harp.'

He put the harp down for a pillow and went to sleep.
The bird of his soul escaped! Free of the body
and the grieving, flying in a vast simple region
that was itself, where it could sing its truth.

'I love this having no head, this tasting without mouth,
this memory without regret, how without hands I gather
rose and basil on an infinitely stretching-out plain
that is my joy.' So this waterbird plunged into its ocean,

Job's fountain where Job was healed of all afflictions,
the pure sunrise. If this *Mathnawi* were suddenly sky,
it could not hold half the mystery that this old poet
was enjoying in sleep. If there were a clear way
into that, no one would stay here!

The Caliph Omar, meanwhile, was napping nearby,
and a voice came, 'Give seven hundred gold dinars
to the man sleeping in the cemetery.'

Everyone understands this voice when it comes.
It speaks with the same authority to Turk and Kurd,
Persian, Arab, Ethiopian, one language!

Omar went to the place and sat by the sleeping man.
Omar sneezed, and the poet sprang up thinking
this great man was there to accuse him.

'No. Sit here beside me. I have a secret to tell you.
There is gold enough in this sack to buy new silk
strings for your instrument. Take it,
buy them, and come back here.'

The old poet heard and realized the generosity
that had come. He threw the harp on the ground
and broke it. 'These songs, breath by breath,

have kept me minding the musical modes of Iraq
and the rhythms of Persia. The minor *zirafgand*,
the liquid freshness of the twenty-four melodies,

these have distracted me while caravan after caravan
was leaving! My poems have kept me in my self,
which was the greatest gift to me, that now
I surrender back.'

                    When someone is counting out
gold for you, don't look at your hands,
or the gold. Look at the giver.

'But even this wailing recrimination,' said Omar,
'is just another shape for enclosure, another joint
on the reed. Pierce the segments and be hollow,
with perforated walls, so flute music can happen.

Don't be a searcher wrapped in the importance of his quest.
Repent of your repenting!' The old man's heart
woke, no longer in love with treble
and bass, without weeping

or laughter. In the true bewilderment of the soul
he went out beyond any seeking, beyond words
and telling, drowned in the beauty,
drowned beyond deliverance.

Waves cover the old man.

Nothing more can be said of him.

He has shaken out his robe,
and there's nothing in it anymore.

There is a chase where a falcon dives into the forest
and doesn't come back up. Every moment,
the sunlight is totally empty
and totally full.

An Egypt That Doesn't Exist

I want to say words that flame
as I say them, but I keep quiet and don't try
to make both worlds fit in one mouthful.

I keep secret in myself an Egypt
that doesn't exist.
Is that good or bad? I don't know.

For years I gave away sexual love
with my eyes. Now I don't.
I'm not in any one place. I don't have a name
for what I give away. Whatever Shams
gave, that you can have from me.

Chinese Art and Greek Art

The Prophet said, 'There are some who see me
by the same light in which I am seeing them.
Our natures are one.
                        Without reference to any strands
of lineage, without reference to texts or traditions,
we drink the life-water together.'
                        Here's a story
about that hidden mystery:
                        The Chinese and the Greeks

were arguing as to who were the better artists.
The king said,
                    'We'll settle this matter with a debate.'
The Chinese began talking,
but the Greeks wouldn't say anything.
They left.
            The Chinese suggested then
that they each be given a room to work on
with their artistry, two rooms facing each other
and divided by a curtain.
                    The Chinese asked the king
for a hundred colors, all the variations,
and each morning they came to where
the dyes were kept and took them all.
The Greeks took no colors.
'They're not part of our work.'
                            They went to their room
and began cleaning and polishing the walls. All day
every day they made those walls as pure and clear
as an open sky.
                There is a way that leads from all-colors
to colorlessness. Know that the magnificent variety
of the clouds and the weather comes from
the total simplicity of the sun and the moon.

The Chinese finished, and they were so happy.
They beat the drums in the joy of completion.

The king entered their room,
astonished by the gorgeous color and detail.

The Greeks then pulled the curtain dividing the rooms.
The Chinese figures and images shimmeringly reflected
on the clear Greek walls. They lived there,
even more beautifully, and always
changing in the light.

The Greek art is the sufi way.
They don't study books of philosophical thought.

They make their loving clearer and clearer.
No wantings, no anger. In that purity
they receive and reflect the images of every moment,
from here, from the stars, from the void.

They take them in
as though they were seeing
with the lighted clarity
that sees them.

*   *   *   *

In your light I learn how to love.
In your beauty, how to make poems.

You dance inside my chest,
where no one sees you,

but sometimes I do,
and that sight becomes this art.

*   *   *   *

Drumsound rises on the air,
its throb, my heart.

A voice inside the beat says,
'I know you're tired,
but come. This is the way.'

*   *   *   *

Are you jealous of the ocean's generosity?
Why would you refuse to give
this joy to anyone?

Fish don't hold the sacred liquid in cups!
They swim the huge fluid freedom.

3. Union:

Gnats Inside the Wind

ON UNION

There is a great feminine wisdom in these poems, a *jemal* quality as opposed to *jelal*. Many of the images of what it's like to be in union have this tone to them. A baby at the mother's breast. A river moving inside the personal fish, taking it to the ocean. Gnats lost in the wind. A dead donkey that has completely melded with a salt flat. The archery champion who lets the arrow fall where he stands. These are not heroic questing images.

What is it to praise? *Be particles.*

During a night of tornadic wind and lightning-everywhere weather in north Georgia, a friend murmured, 'Where do hummingbirds go in this?' The next morning the hummingbirds, the same ones, were back fussing at the feeder. They know a hiding trick the gnats don't. I think sometimes that poems can be places to hide, opisthodamal robe closets simulating the experiences they celebrate.

What is the soul? *Consciousness.*

Gnats Inside the Wind

Some gnats come from the grass to speak with Solomon.

'O Solomon, you are the champion of the oppressed.
You give justice to the little guys, and they don't get
any littler than us! We are tiny metaphors
for frailty. Can you defend us?'

'Who has mistreated you?'

'Our complaint is against the wind.'

'Well,' says Solomon, 'you have pretty voices,
you gnats, but remember, a judge cannot listen
to just one side. I must hear both litigants.'

'Of course,' agree the gnats.

'Summon the East Wind!' calls out Solomon,
and the wind arrives almost immediately.

What happened to the gnat plaintiffs? Gone.

Such is the way of every seeker who comes to complain
at the High Court. When the presence of God arrives,
where are the seekers? First there's dying,
then union, like gnats inside the wind.

Meadowsounds

We've come again to that knee of seacoast
no ocean can reach.

Tie together all human intellects.
They won't stretch to here.

The sky bares its neck so beautifully,
but gets no kiss. Only a taste.

This is the food that everyone wants,
wandering the wilderness, 'Please give us
your manna and quail.'

We're here again with the beloved.
This air, a shout. These meadowsounds,
an astonishing myth.

We've come into the presence of the one
who was never apart from us.

When the waterbag is filling, you know
the water carrier's here!

The bag leans lovingly against your shoulder.
'Without you I have no knowledge,
no way to touch anyone.'

When someone chews sugarcane,
he's wanting this sweetness.

Inside this globe the soul roars like thunder.
And now silence, my strict tutor.

I won't try to talk about Shams.
Language cannot touch that presence.

Ayaz and the King's Pearl

One day the king assembled his courtiers.
He handed the minister a glowing pearl.
'What would you say this is worth?'
                                      'More gold
than a hundred donkeys could carry.'
                                      'Break it!'
'Sir, how could I waste your resources
like that?' The king presented him
with a robe of honor for his answer

and took back the pearl. He talked awhile
to the assembly on various topics.

                      Then he put the pearl

in the chamberlain's hand. 'What would it sell for?'
'Half a kingdom, God preserve it!'
                         'Break it!'
'My hand could not move to do such a thing.'
The king rewarded him with a robe of honor
and an increase in his salary, and so it went
with each of the fifty or sixty courtiers.

One by one, they imitated the minister
and the chamberlain and received new wealth.

Then the pearl was given to Ayaz.

'Can you say how splendid this is?'
'It's more than I can say.'
                      'Then break it,
this second, into tiny pieces.'
                      Ayaz had had a dream
about this, and he'd hidden two stones in his sleeve.
He crushed the pearl to powder between them.

As Joseph at the bottom of the well listened
to the end of his story, so such listeners
understand success and un-success as one thing.

Don't worry about forms.
If someone wants your horse,
let him have it. Horses are for
hurrying ahead of the others.

The court assembly screamed at the recklessness
of Ayaz, 'How could you do that?'

'What the king says is worth more than any pearl.
I honor the king, not some coloured stone.'

The princes immediately fell on their knees
and put their foreheads on the ground.

Their sighs went up like a smoke cloud
asking forgiveness. The king gestured
to his executioner as though to say,
'Take out this trash.'
                              Ayaz sprang forward.
'Your mercy makes them bow like this.
Give them their lives! Let them keep hoping
for union with you. They see their forgetfulness
now, as the drunken man did when he said,
"I didn't know what I was doing," and then
someone pointed out, "But you invited
that forgetfulness into you. You drank it.
There was a choice!"

They know deeply now how imitation
lulled them to sleep. Don't separate yourself
from them. Look at all their heads against the floor.

Raise their faces into yours. Let them wash
in your cool washing place.'

Ayaz and his speech always get to this point
and then the pen breaks. How can a saucer
contain the ocean? The drunks break their cups,
but you poured that wine!
                              Ayaz said, 'You picked me
to crush the pearl. Don't punish the others
for my drunken obedience!
Punish them when I'm sober,
because I'll never be sober again.

Whoever bows down like they are bowing down
will not rise up in his old self again.

Like a gnat in your buttermilk,
they've become your buttermilk.

The mountains are trembling. Their map and compass
are the lines in your palm.'
Husam,
I need a hundred mouths to say this,
but I only have this one!

A hundred thousand impressions from the spirit
are wanting to come through here.
I feel stunned
in this abundance, crushed and dead.

Put This Design in Your Carpet

Spiritual experience is a modest woman
who looks lovingly at only one man.

It's a great river where ducks
live happily, and crows drown.

The visible bowl of form contains food
that is both nourishing and a source of heartburn.

There is an unseen presence we honor
that gives the gifts.

You're water. We're the millstone.
You're wind. We're dust blown up into shapes.
You're spirit. We're the opening and closing

of our hands. You're the clarity.
We're this language that tries to say it.
You're joy. We're all the different kinds of laughing.

Any movement or sound is a profession of faith,
as the millstone grinding is explaining how it believes
in the river! No metaphor can say this,
but I can't stop pointing
to the beauty.

Every moment and place says,
'Put this design in your carpet!'

Like the shepherd in Book II,
who wanted to pick the lice off God's robe,
and stitch up God's shoes, I want to be
in such a passionate adoration
that my tent gets pitched against the sky!

Let the beloved come
and sit like a guard dog
in front of the tent.

When the ocean surges,
don't let me just hear it.
Let it splash inside my chest!

Hallaj

Hallaj said what he said and went to the origin
through the hole in the scaffold.

I cut a cap's worth of cloth from his robe,
and it swamped over me from head to foot.

Years ago, I broke a bunch of roses
from the top of his wall. A thorn from that
is still in my palm, working deeper.

From Hallaj, I learned to hunt lions,
but I became something hungrier than a lion.

I was a frisky colt. He broke me
with a quiet hand on the side of my head.

A person comes to him naked. It's cold.
There's a fur coat floating in the river.

'Jump in and get it,' he says.
You dive in. You reach for the coat.
It reaches for you.

It's a live bear that has fallen in upstream,
drifting with the current.

'How long does it take!' Hallaj yells from the bank.
'Don't wait,' you answer. 'This coat
has decided to wear me home!'

A little part of a story, a hint.
Do you need long sermons on Hallaj!

We Three

My love wanders the rooms, melodious,
flute notes, plucked wires,
full of a wine the Magi drank
on the way to Bethlehem.

We are three. The moon comes
from its quiet corner, puts a pitcher of water
down in the center. The circle
of surface flames.

One of us kneels to kiss the threshold.

One drinks, with wine-flames playing over his face.

One watches the gathering,
and says to any cold onlookers,

>   *This dance is the joy of existence.*

*   *   *   *

I am filled with you.
Skin, blood, bone, brain, and soul.
There's no room for lack of trust, or trust.
Nothing in this existence but that existence.

4. The Sheikh:

I Have Such a Teacher

ON THE SHEIKH

The existence of the beloved is not provable, nor is it fantasy. The Friend, as Rumi usually calls this presence within and infinitely beyond the senses, is elusive and nearer than the big vein on your neck; you need a mirror to see it. The sheikh is a mirror, a reminder of that presence, and a cook. The understanding that comes through a sheikh gives nourishment and transforming energy to many. Rumi's image of a disciple is a chickpea that sprouts and enjoys the rainy garden of sexual pleasure. It matures to its hardened form, then gets picked and thrown in the cooking pot. The cook's tending is careful and constant and, in Rumi's case, garrulous. Gradually the disciple softens and takes on flavors the cook adds. Eventually he or she becomes tasty enough to be appealing to those who in the sufi tradition are called the True Human Beings. So the chickpea moves from garden to cooking pot to a taste for the cook, finally to become sustenance for a mysterious community.

Chickpea to Cook

A chickpea leaps almost over the rim of the pot
where it's being boiled.

'Why are you doing this to me?'

The cook knocks him down with the ladle.

'Don't you try to jump out.
You think I'm torturing you.
I'm giving you flavor,
so you can mix with spices and rice
and be the lovely vitality of a human being.

Remember when you drank rain in the garden.
That was for this.'

Grace first. Sexual pleasure,
then a boiling new life begins,
and the Friend has something good to eat.

Eventually the chickpea
will say to the cook,
                              'Boil me some more.
Hit me with the skimming spoon.
I can't do this by myself.

I'm like an elephant that dreams of gardens
back in Hindustan and doesn't pay attention
to his driver. You're my cook, my driver,
my way into existence. I love your cooking.'

The cook says,
                              'I was once like you,
fresh from the ground. Then I boiled in time,
and boiled in the body, two fierce boilings.

My animal soul grew powerful.
I controlled it with practices,
and boiled some more, and boiled
once beyond that,
                              and became your teacher.'

I Have Such a Teacher

Last night my teacher taught me the lesson of poverty,
having nothing and wanting nothing.

I am a naked man standing inside a mine of rubies,
clothed in red silk.
I absorb the shining and now I see the ocean,
billions of simultaneous motions
moving in me.
A circle of lovely, quiet people
becomes the ring on my finger.

Then the wind and thunder of rain on the way.
I have such a teacher.

Sublime Generosity

I was dead, then alive.
Weeping, then laughing.

The power of love came into me,
and I became fierce like a lion,
then tender like the evening star.

He said, 'You're not mad enough.
You don't belong in this house.'

I went wild and had to be tied up.
He said, 'Still not wild enough
to stay with us!'

I broke through another layer
into joyfulness.

He said, 'It's not enough.'
I died.

He said, 'You're a clever little man,
full of fantasy and doubting.'

I plucked out my feathers and became a fool.
He said, 'Now you're the candle
for this assembly.'

But I'm no candle. Look!
I'm scattered smoke.

He said, 'You are the sheikh, the guide.'
But I'm not a teacher. I have no power.

He said, 'You already have wings.
I cannot give you wings.'

But I wanted *his* wings.
I felt like some flightless chicken.

Then new events said to me,
'Don't move. A sublime generosity is
coming toward you.'

And old love said, 'Stay with me.'

I said, 'I will.'

You are the fountain of the sun's light.
I am a willow shadow on the ground.
You make my raggedness silky.

The soul at dawn is like darkened water
that slowly begins to say *Thank you, thank you.*

Then at sunset, again, Venus gradually
changes into the moon and then the whole nightsky.

This comes of smiling back
at your smile.

The chess master says nothing,
other than moving the silent chess piece.

That I am part of the ploys
of this game makes me
amazingly happy.

Like This

If anyone asks you
how the perfect satisfaction
of all our sexual wanting
will look, lift your face
and say,
>   *Like this.*

When someone mentions the gracefulness
of the nightsky, climb up on the roof
and dance and say,
>   *Like this?*

If anyone wants to know what 'spirit' is,
or what 'God's fragrance' means,
lean your head toward him or her.
Keep your face there close.
>   *Like this.*

When someone quotes the old poetic image
about clouds gradually uncovering the moon,
slowly loosen knot by knot the strings
of your robe.
>   *Like this?*

If anyone wonders how Jesus raised the dead,
don't try to explain the miracle.
Kiss me on the lips.
>   *Like this. Like this.*

When someone asks what it means
to 'die for love,' point
>   *here.*

If someone asks how tall I am, frown
and measure with your fingers the space
between the creases on your forehead.
>   *This tall.*

The soul sometimes leaves the body, then returns.
When someone doesn't believe that,
walk back into my house.
>   *Like this.*

When lovers moan,
they're telling our story.
>   *Like this.*

I am a sky where spirits live.
Stare into this deepening blue,
while the breeze says a secret.
>   *Like this.*

When someone asks what there is to do,
light the candle in his hand.

> *Like this.*

How did Joseph's scent come to Jacob?

> *Huuuuu.*

How did Jacob's sight return?

> *Huuuu.*

A little wind cleans the eyes.

> *Like this.*

When Shams comes back from Tabriz,
he'll put just his head around the edge
of the door to surprise us.

> *Like this.*

A Bowl

Imagine the time the particle you are
returns where it came from!

The family darling comes home. Wine,
without being contained in cups,
is handed around.

A red glint appears in a granite outcrop,
and suddenly the whole cliff turns to ruby.

At dawn I walked along with a monk
on his way to the monastery.

> 'We do the same work,'

I told him. 'We suffer the same.'

He gave me a bowl.
And I saw:
   the soul has *this* shape.
                      Shams,
you that teach us and actual sunlight,
                             help me now,

being in the middle of being partly in my self,
and partly outside.

Wax

When I see you and how you are,
I close my eyes to the other.
For your Solomon's seal I become wax
throughout my body. I wait to be light.
I give up opinions on all matters.
I become the reed flute for your breath.

You were inside my hand.
I kept reaching around for something.
I was inside your hand, but I kept asking questions
of those who know very little.

I must have been incredibly simple or drunk or insane
to sneak into my own house and steal money,
to climb over the fence and take my own vegetables.
But no more. I've gotten free of that ignorant fist
that was pinching and twisting my secret self.

The universe and the light of the stars come through me.
I am the crescent moon put up
over the gate to the festival.

No Room for Form

On the night when you cross the street
from your shop and your house
to the cemetery,

you'll hear me hailing you from inside
the open grave, and you'll realize
how we've always been together.

I am the clear consciousness-core
of your being, the same in
ecstasy as in self-hating fatigue.

That night, when you escape the fear of snakebite
and all irritation with the ants, you'll hear
my familiar voice, see the candle being lit,
smell the incense, the surprise meal fixed
by the lover inside all your other lovers.

This heart-tumult is my signal
to you igniting in the tomb.

So don't fuss with the shroud
and the graveyard road dust.

Those get ripped open and washed away
in the music of our finally meeting.

And don't look for me in a human shape.
I am inside your looking. No room
for form with love this strong.

Beat the drum and let the poets speak.
This is a day of purification for those who
are already mature and initiated into what love is.

No need to wait until we die!
There's more to want here than money
and being famous and bites of roasted meat.

Now, what shall we call this new sort of gazing-house
that has opened in our town where people sit
quietly and pour out their glancing
like light, like answering?

Childhood Friends

You may have heard, it's the custom for kings
to let warriors stand on the left, the side of the heart,
and courage. On the right they put the chancellor,
and various secretaries, because the practice
of bookkeeping and writing usually belongs
to the right hand. In the center,
                                    the sufis,
because in meditation they become mirrors.
The king can look at their faces
and see his original state.

Give the beautiful ones mirrors,
and let them fall in love with themselves.

That way they polish their souls
and kindle remembering in others.

A close childhood friend once came to visit Joseph.
They had shared the secrets that children tell each other
when they're lying on their pillows at night
before they go to sleep. These two
were completely truthful
with each other.

The friend asked, 'What was it like when you realized
your brothers were jealous and what they planned to do?'

'I felt like a lion with a chain around its neck.
Not degraded by the chain, and not complaining,
but just waiting for my power to be recognized.'

'How about down in the well, and in prison?
How was it then?'
                      'Like the moon when it's getting
smaller, yet knowing the fullness to come.
Like a seed pearl ground in the mortar for medicine,
that knows it will now be the light in a human eye.

Like a wheat grain that breaks open in the ground,
then grows, then gets harvested, then crushed in the mill
for flour, then baked, then crushed again between teeth
to become a person's deepest understanding.
Lost in love, like the songs the planters sing
the night after they sow the seed.'
                      There is no end
to any of this.
              Back to something else the good man
and Joseph talked about.
                      'Ah my friend, what have you
brought me? You know a traveler should not arrive
empty-handed at the door of a friend like me.
That's going to the grinding stone without your wheat.

God will ask at the resurrection, "Did you bring Me
a present? Did you forget? Did you think
you wouldn't see me?" '
                              Joseph kept teasing,
'Let's have it. I want my gift!'

The guest began, 'You can't imagine how I've looked
for something for you. Nothing seemed appropriate.
You don't take gold down into a goldmine,
or a drop of water to the Sea of Oman!
Everything I thought of was like bringing cumin seed
to Kirmanshah where cumin comes from.

You have all seeds in your barn. You even have my love
and my soul, so I can't even bring those.

I've brought you a mirror. Look at yourself,
and remember me.'
                              He took the mirror out from his robe
where he was hiding it.
                              What is the mirror of being?
Non-being. Always bring a mirror of non-existence
as a gift. Any other present is foolish.

Let the poor man look deep into generosity.
Let bread see a hungry man.
Let kindling behold a spark from the flint.

An empty mirror and your worst destructive habits,
when they are held up to each other,
that's when the real making begins.
That's what art and crafting are.

A tailor needs a torn garment to practice his expertise.
The trunks of trees must be cut and cut again
so they can be used for fine carpentry.

Your doctor must have a broken leg to doctor.
Your defects are the ways that glory gets manifested.
Whoever sees clearly what's diseased in himself
begins to gallop on the way.

There is nothing worse
than thinking you are well enough.
More than anything, self-complacency
blocks the workmanship.

Put your vileness up to a mirror and weep.
Get that self-satisfaction flowing out of you!
Satan thought, 'I am better than Adam,'
and that *better than* is still strongly in us.

Your stream water may look clean,
but there's unstirred matter on the bottom.
Your sheikh can dig a side channel
that will drain that waste off.

Trust your wound to a teacher's surgery.
Flies collect on a wound. They cover it,
those flies of your self-protecting feelings,
your love for what you think is yours.

Let a teacher wave away the flies
and put a plaster on the wound.

Don't turn your head. Keep looking
at the bandaged place. That's where
the light enters you.
                    And don't believe for a moment
that you're healing yourself.

The Mouse and the Camel

A mouse caught hold of a camel's lead rope
in his two forelegs and walked off with it,
imitating the camel drivers.

> The camel went along,
letting the mouse feel heroic.

> 'Enjoy yourself,'
he thought. 'I have something to teach you, presently.'

They came to the edge of a great river.
The mouse was dumbfounded.

> 'What are you waiting for?
Step forward into the river. You are my leader.
Don't stop here.'

> 'I'm afraid of being drowned.'

The camel walked into the water. 'It's only
just above the knee.'

> '*Your* knee! Your knee
is a hundred times over my head!'

> 'Well, maybe you shouldn't
be leading a camel. Stay with those like yourself.
A mouse has nothing really to say to a camel.'

'Would you help me get across?'

'Get up on my hump. I am made to take hundreds like you across.'

You are not a prophet, but go humbly on the way of the prophets,

and you can arrive where they are. Don't try to steer the boat.
Don't open a shop by yourself. Listen. Keep silent.
You are not God's mouthpiece. Try to be an ear,
and if you do speak, ask for explanations.

The source of your arrogance and anger is your lust
and the rootedness of that is in your habits.

Someone who makes a habit of eating clay
gets mad when you try to keep him from it.
Being a leader can also be a poisonous habit,
so that when someone questions your authority,
you think, 'He's trying to take over.'
You may respond courteously, but inside you rage.

Always check your inner state
with the lord of your heart.
Copper doesn't know it's copper,
until it's changed to gold.

Your loving doesn't know its majesty,
until it knows its helplessness.

*   *   *   *

These gifts from the Friend, a robe
of skin and veins, a teacher within,
wear them and become a school,
with a greater sheikh nearby.

*   *   *   *

The Lame Goat

You've seen a herd of goats
going down to the water.

The lame and dreamy goat
brings up the rear.

There are worried faces about that one,
but now they're laughing,

because look, as they return,
that goat is leading!

There are many different kinds of knowing.
The lame goat's kind is a branch
that traces back to the roots of presence.

Learn from the lame goat,
and lead the herd home.

5. *Recognizing Elegance:*

Your Reasonable Father

ON ELEGANCE

The sudden opening of one's eyes to the elaborate, extravagant beauty around us. Watching Madagascan meerkats on the Discovery channel. The gorgeous dirt road down to the river. Three hundred million galaxies. The gold around a frog's eye. The intricacy of the present moment, all the wealth we need. Rumi feels this abundance, and his gratitude for it pours out the waterfall of his work.

It may be that the clarity Rumi calls 'reason' is a brilliant lawfulness that ecologists and astronomers examine as the coherence in any system, and that the mystic and the scientist both attend the same layered intelligence: the grand and precise artistry of existence.

Father Reason

The universe is a form of divine law,
your reasonable father.

When you feel ungrateful to him,
the shapes of the world seem mean and ugly.

Make peace with that father, the elegant patterning,
and every experience will fill with immediacy.

Because I love this, I am never bored.
Beauty constantly wells up, a noise of springwater
in my ear and in my inner being.

Tree limbs rise and fall like the ecstatic arms
of those who have submitted to the mystical life.

Leaf sounds talk together like poets
making fresh metaphors. The green felt cover slips,
and we get a flash of the mirror underneath.

Think how it will be when the whole thing
is pulled away! I tell only one one-thousandth
of what I see, because there's so much doubt everywhere.

The conventional opinion of this poetry is,
it shows great optimism for the future.

But Father Reason says,
No need to announce the future!
This now is it. *This.* Your deepest need and desire
is satisfied by the *moment's* energy
here in your hand.

*   *   *   *

A craftsman pulled a reed from the reedbed,
cut holes in it, and called it a human being.

Since then, it's been wailing a tender agony
of parting, never mentioning the skill
that gave it life as a flute.

*   *   *   *

Humble living does not diminish. It fills.
Going back to a simpler self gives wisdom.

When a man makes up a story for his child,
he becomes a father and a child
together, listening.

*   *   *   *

New Moon, Hilal

You've heard about the qualities of Bilal.
Now hear about the thinness of Hilal,
which is more advanced than Bilal.

He denied his *nafs* more than some of you
who move backward, from being an illumined globe
toward becoming again an opaque stone.

Remember the story of the young guest
who came before a certain king. 'And how old are you,
my lad? Tell the truth now. Say it out.'

'Eighteen, well seventeen.   Sixteen.
Actually, uh, fifteen.'

'Keep going! You'll end up
in your mother's womb.'

Or the man who went to borrow a horse.
'Take the gray.'
                    'No, not that one.'
'Why?'
          'It goes in reverse. It backs up.'

'Then turn its tail toward your home.'

The beast you ride is your various appetites.
Change your wantings. When you prune
weak branches, the remaining fruit
get tastier. Lust can be redirected,
so that even when it takes you backward,
it goes toward shelter.

A strong intention can make 'two oceans wide'
be the size of a blanket, or 'seven hundred years'
the time it takes to walk to someone you love.

True seekers keep riding straight through,
whereas big, lazy, self-worshiping geese
unload their pack animals in a farmyard
and say, 'This is far enough.'

Do you know the story of the travelers
who came to a village in early Spring?
There's an abandoned house with an open door.

'Why don't we wait for this cold spell to pass,
this *old woman's chill*, they call it.
Let's put our baggage in here and rest.'

A deep voice from inside, 'No. Unload outside,
then enter. This is a meeting hall
of great dignity!'

There are such secret sanctuaries.

Although he worked in a stable as a groom,
Hilal was an enlightened master.

His employer did not understand Hilal's state.
He knew up and down and north–south–east–west,
the evidence of the senses, but nothing else.

The color of the ground is in front of us,
but prophetic light is hidden.

One person sees a minaret, but not the bird
perched there. A second person sees the bird,
but not the hair it carries. A third
sees minaret, bird, and hair.

Until you can see the thread of the hair,
the knot of awareness will not be loosened.

The body is the minaret. Obedience,
the bird. Or three hundred birds, or two,
however you want it. The second person
sees the bird, and only the bird.

The hair is the secret
that belongs to the bird.

No nest built with such material
will go unused. A song-thread flows
continuously out of the bird.

Try to see this bird on its clay tower,
and also the hair floating in its beak.

Hilal becomes ill. Nine days he lies sick
in the stable. No one notices,
except the prophet Muhammad, peace
and blessing be upon him.
He comes to visit.

Hilal's employer is ecstatic.
With elaborate ceremony he emerges
from his upstairs room and kisses the ground
in front of the Prophet. 'In God's name,
please honor this house.'

'I'm not here to visit you.'

'Who then?'

'There is a new-moon new-man planted near here,
spending the lightness of his humility
like blossoms on the ground.
Where is Hilal?'

'I haven't seen him for days.
He must be out with the mules and the horses.'

Muhammad runs to the stable. It's dark,
and the stench of manure is strong,
but all that vanishes when friendship enters.

Miracles don't cause faith, but rather
the scent of kindredness that unites people.

Miracles overwhelm unbelief.
Faith grows from friendship.

With the familiar fragrance, Hilal wakes up.
How could such a thing be in a stable?

Through the legs of the horses he sees
the robes of Muhammad! He comes crawling out
from the dark corner and lays his cheek
on Muhammad's feet. Muhammad puts his cheek
on Hilal's and kisses his head and face.

Recognizing Elegance   49

'How hidden can one be!
Are you better? How are you?'
                    HOW!

A man sits and eats damp clay for moisture.
How is it with him when a flood of fresh
prophetic rainwater suddenly rides him along?

How is it when a blind, filthy dog wakes up,
and finds that he's a lion, and not
a lion such as could be killed,
but a spirit-lion who shatters sword
and javelin with just his presence?

How would that feel? A man crawls for years
on his stomach with his eyes closed.
Then one moment he opens his eyes,
and he's in a garden. It's Spring.

How is to be free of HOW,
loose in howlessness?

Howlers sit waiting around your table.
Throw them a bone!

This suggestion: wash before going to the watertank.
The waters there have grace enough to clean
and give you peace, but wash yourself
of *hows* before you go.

Wash off all wonderings-why
and workings-out-however.
Don't take those with you
to the big watertank.

Husam! Bats don't bother Husamuddin.
He's an expert on sunlight!

He's written about the new moon, Hilal.
Now he'll write about the full moon, the sheikh.
New moon and full moon are the same.

A new moon teaches gradualness
and deliberation and how one gives birth
to oneself slowly. Patience with small details
makes perfect a large work, like the universe.

What nine months of attention does for an embryo
forty early mornings will do
for your gradually growing wholeness.

Body Intelligence

Your intelligence is always with you,
overseeing your body, even though
you may not be aware of its work.

If you start doing something against
your health, your intelligence
will eventually scold you.

If it hadn't been so lovingly close by,
and so constantly monitoring,
how could it rebuke?

You and your intelligence
are like the beauty and the precision
of an astrolabe.

Together, you calculate how near
existence is to the sun!

Your intelligence is marvelously intimate.
It's not in front of you or behind,
or to the left or the right.

Now try, my friend, to describe how near
is the creator of your intellect!

Intellectual searching will not find
the way to that king!

The movement of your finger
is not separate from your finger.

You go to sleep, or you die,
and there's no intelligent motion.

Then you wake,
and your fingers
fill with meanings.

Now consider the jewel-lights
in your eyes. How do *they* work?

This visible universe has many weathers
and variations.
                  But uncle, O uncle,
the universe of the creation-word,
the divine command to *Be*, that universe
of qualities is beyond any pointing to.

More intelligent than intellect,
and more spiritual than spirit.

No being is unconnected
to that reality, and that connection
cannot be said. *There*, there's
no separation and no return.

There are guides who can show you the way.
Use them. But they will not satisfy your longing.

Keep wanting that connection
with all your pulsing energy.

The throbbing vein
will take you further
than any thinking.

Muhammad said, 'Don't theorize
about essence!' All speculations
are just more layers of covering.
Human beings love coverings!

They think the designs on the curtains
are what's being concealed.

Observe the wonders as they occur around you.
Don't claim them. Feel the artistry
moving through, and be silent.

Or say, 'I cannot praise You
as You should be praised.

Such words are infinitely
beyond my understanding.'

The Seed Market

Can you find another market like this?

Where,
with your one rose
you can buy hundreds of rose gardens?

Where,
for one seed
you get a whole wilderness?

For one weak breath,
the divine wind?

You've been fearful
of being absorbed in the ground,
or drawn up by the air.

Now, your waterbead lets go
and drops into the ocean,
where it came from.

It no longer has the form it had,
but it's still water.
The essence is the same.

This giving up is not a repenting.
It's a deep honoring of yourself.

When the ocean comes to you as a lover,
marry, at once, quickly,
for God's sake!

Don't postpone it!
Existence has no better gift.

No amount of searching
will find this.

A perfect falcon, for no reason,
has landed on your shoulder,
and become yours.

6. The Howling Necessity:

Cry Out in Your Weakness

ON HOWLING

My sufi teacher, Bawa Muhaiyaddeen, when he saw me, and knowing my name was Barks, would go into a wolf howl for a joke and a teaching. He mirrored some need to howl that he saw there walking in. He himself would often break into spontaneous praise songs while sitting on his bed. Crying out loud for help is Rumi's point. With that vulnerable breaking open in the psyche, the milk of grace starts to flow.

Love Dogs

One night a man was crying,
                              Allah! Allah!
His lips grew sweet with the praising,
until a cynic said,
                    'So! I have heard you
calling out, but have you ever
gotten any response?'

The man had no answer to that.
He quit praying and fell into a confused sleep.

He dreamed he saw Khidr, the guide of souls,
in a thick, green foliage.
                              'Why did you stop praising?'

'Because I never heard anything back.'

'This longing
you express *is* the return message.'

The grief you cry out from
draws you toward union.

Your pure sadness
that wants help
is the secret cup.

Listen to the moan of a dog for its master.
That whining is the connection.

There are love dogs
no one knows the names of.

Give your life
to be one of them.

Cry Out in Your Weakness

A dragon was pulling a bear into its terrible mouth.

A courageous man went and rescued the bear.
There are such helpers in the world, who rush to save
anyone who cries out. Like Mercy itself,
they run toward the screaming.

And they can't be bought off.
If you were to ask one of those, 'Why did you come
so quickly?' he or she would say, 'Because I heard
your helplessness.'

Where lowland is,

that's where water goes. All medicine wants
is pain to cure.
                    And don't just ask for one mercy.
Let them flood in. Let the sky open under your feet.
Take the cotton out of your ears, the cotton
of consolations, so you can hear the sphere-music.

Push the hair out of your eyes.
Blow the phlegm from your nose,
and from your brain.

Let the wind breeze through.
Leave no residue in yourself from that bilious fever.
Take the cure for impotence,
that your manhood may shoot forth,
and a hundred new beings come of your coming.

Tear the binding from around the foot
of your soul, and let it race around the track
in front of the crowd. Loosen the knot of greed
so tight on your neck. Accept your new good luck.

Give your weakness
to one who helps.

Crying out loud and weeping are great resources.
A nursing mother, all she does
is wait to hear her child.

Just a little beginning-whimper,
and she's there.

God created the child, that is, your wanting,
so that it might cry out, so that milk might come.

Cry out! Don't be stolid and silent
with your pain. Lament! And let the milk
of loving flow into you.

The hard rain and wind
are ways the cloud has
to take care of us.

Be patient.
Respond to every call
that excites your spirit.

Ignore those that make you fearful
and sad, that degrade you
back toward disease and death.

The Debtor Sheikh

Sheikh Ahmad was continually in debt.
He borrowed great sums from the wealthy
and gave it out to the poor dervishes of the world.
He built a sufi monastery by borrowing,
and God was always paying his debts, turning sand
into flour for this generous friend.

The Prophet said that there were always two angels
praying in the market. One said, 'Lord,
give the poor wanderer help.' The other, 'Lord,
give the miser a poison.' Especially loud
is the former prayer when the wanderer is a prodigal
like Sheikh Ahmad, the debtor sheikh.

For years, until his death, he scattered seed profusely.
Even very near his death, with the signs of death clear,
he sat surrounded by creditors. The creditors in a circle,
and the great sheikh in the center gently melting
into himself like a candle.

The creditors were so sour-faced with worry
that they could hardly breathe.

'Look at these despairing men,' thought the sheikh.
'Do they think God does not have four hundred gold dinars?'
Just at that moment a boy outside called,

                                    'Halvah, a sixth
of a dirhem for a piece! Fresh halvah!'

                        Sheikh Ahmad,
with a nod of his head, directed the famulus
to go and buy the whole tray of halvah.

'Maybe if these creditors eat a little sweetness,
they won't look so bitterly on me.'

The servant went to the boy, 'How much for the whole lump
of halvah?'

                'Half a dinar, and some change.'

'Don't ask too much from sufis, my son.
Half a dinar is enough.'

The boy handed over the tray, and the servant brought it
to the sheikh, who passed it among his creditor guests.
'Please, eat, and be happy.'

The tray was quickly emptied, and the boy asked the sheikh
for his half a gold dinar.

'Where would I find such money? These men can tell you
how in debt I am, and besides, I am fast on my way
into non-existence.'

The boy threw the tray on the floor
and started weeping loud and yelling,

'I wish
I had broken my legs before I came in here!

I wish
I'd stayed in the bathhouse today. You gluttonous,
plate-licking sufis, washing your faces like cats!'

A crowd gathered. The boy continued, 'Oh sheikh,
my master will beat me if I come back without anything.'

The creditors joined in, 'How could you do this?
You've devoured our properties, and now you add this
one last debt before you die.

Why?'

The sheikh closes his eyes and does not answer.
The boy weeps until afternoon prayers. The sheikh
withdraws underneath his coverlet,

pleased with everything,
pleased with eternity, pleased with death,

and totally
unconcerned with all the reviling talk around him.

On a bright-moon night, do you think the moon,
cruising through the tenth house, can hear the dogs barking
down here?

But the dogs are doing what they're supposed to do.
Water does not lose its purity because of a bit of weed
floating in it.

That king drinks wine on the riverbank
until dawn, listening to the water music, not hearing

the frog talk.
                    The money due the boy would have been
just a few pennies from each of his creditors, but the sheikh's
spiritual power prevents that from happening.
No one gives the boy anything.

At afternoon prayers a servant comes with a tray
from Hatim, a friend of Ahmad's, and a man
of great property. A covered tray.

The sheikh uncovers the face of the tray, and on it
there are four hundred gold dinars, and in one corner,
another half a dinar wrapped in a piece of paper.

Immediately the cries of abasement, 'O king of sheikhs,
lord of the lords of mystery! Forgive us.
We were bumbling and crazed. We were knocking lamps over.
We were . . .'
                    'It's all right. You will not be held
responsible for what you've said or done. The secret here
is that I asked God and the way was shown
that until the boy's weeping, God's merciful generosity
was not loosened.
                    Let the boy be like the pupil of your eye.
If you want to wear a robe of spiritual sovereignty,
let your eyes weep with the wanting.'

*   *   *   *

You that come to birth and bring the mysteries,
your voice-thunder makes us very happy.

Roar, lion of the heart,
and tear me open!

7. Teaching Stories:

How the Unseen World Works

ON THE UNSEEN

Ibn Khafif Shirazi tells this story: 'I heard that there were two great masters in Egypt, so I hurried to reach their presence. When I arrived, I saw two magnificent teachers meditating. I greeted them three times, but they did not answer. I meditated with them for four days. Each day I begged them to talk with me, since I had come such a long way. Finally the younger one opened his eyes. "Ibn Khafif, life is short. Use the portion that's left to deepen yourself. Don't waste time greeting people!" I asked him to give me some advice. "Stay in the presence of those who remind you of your lord, who not only speak wisdom, but *are* that." Then he went back into meditation.' Ibn Khafif was being taught the importance of having his own experience of the unseen, and not to fret so much about the forms of greeting people, hearing wisdom, and about what we should be doing.

There is a South Indian story about soap. Soap is the dirt we buy. We introduce it to the dirt we have, and the two dirts are so glad to see each other they come out and mix! They swim together in the warm pleasurable water and, at just the right moment, the washer lifts the cloth of our true being free of both soap and dirt. Mystical poetry and other practices may function this way, as soap that dances with what disturbs our clarity. Then at some moment they drop away and leave us clean, ready to be worn again.

Nasuh

Some time ago there was a man named Nasuh.
He made his living shampooing women in a bathhouse.
He had a face like a woman, but he was not effeminate,
though he disguised his virility, so as to keep his job.

He loved touching the women as he washed their hair.
He stayed sexually alert, at full strength,
all the time, massaging the beautiful women,
especially the Princess and her ladies-in-waiting.

Sometimes he thought of changing jobs,
of doing something
where he wouldn't be so constantly lustful,
but he couldn't quit.

He went to a mystic saint and said,
'Please remember me in a prayer.'

That holy man was spiritually free,
and totally opened to God. He knew Nasuh's secret,
but with God's gentleness he didn't speak it.

A gnostic says little, but inside he is full of mysteries,
and crowded with voices. Whoever is served
that cup keeps quiet.

The holy man laughed softly and prayed aloud,
'May God cause you to change your life
in the way you know you should.'

The prayer of such a sheikh is different
from other prayers. He has so completely dissolved
his ego, nothinged himself, that what he says

is like God talking to God. How could
such a prayer not be granted?

The means were found to change Nasuh.
While he was pouring water into a basin
for a naked woman, she felt and discovered
that a pearl was missing from her earring.

Quickly, they locked the doors.
They searched the cushions, the towels, the rugs,
and the discarded clothes. Nothing.
                                        Now they search
ears and mouths and every cleft and orifice.

Everyone is made to strip,
and the queen's lady chamberlain
probes one by one
the naked women.
                        Nasuh, meanwhile,
has gone to his private closet, trembling.

'I didn't steal the pearl,
but if they undress and search me,
they'll see how excited I get
with these nude ladies.
                        God, please,
help me!
            I have been cold and lecherous,
but cover my sin this time, PLEASE!
Let me not be exposed for how I've been.
I'll repent!'
            He weeps and moans and weeps,
for the moment is upon him.
                        'Nasuh!
We have searched everyone but you. Come out!'

At that moment his spirit grows wings, and lifts.
His ego falls like a battered wall.
He unites with God, alive,
but emptied of
Nasuh.

His ship sinks and in its place move the ocean waves.
His body's disgrace, like a falcon's loosened binding,
slips from the falcon's foot.

His stones drink in water.
His field shines like satin with gold threads in it.
Someone dead a hundred years steps out well
and strong and handsome.
                              A broken stick
breaks into bud.

This all happens inside Nasuh,
after the call that gave him such fear.

A long pause.
A long, waiting silence.

Then a shout from one of the women, 'Here it is!'
The bathhouse fills with clapping.
Nasuh sees his new life sparkling out before him.

The women come to apologize, 'We're so sorry
we didn't trust you. We just knew
that you'd taken that pearl.'

They kept talking about how they'd suspected him,
and begging his forgiveness.

Finally he replies,
                              'I am much more guilty

than anyone has thought or said. I am the worst person
in the world. What you have said is only a hundredth
of what I've actually done. Don't ask my pardon!

You don't know me. No one knows me.
God has hidden my sneakiness. Satan taught me tricks,
but after a time, those became easy, and I taught Satan
some new variations. God saw what I did, but chose
not to publicly reveal my sin.

And now, I am sewn back into wholeness!
Whatever I've done,

>   now was not done.
Whatever obedience I didn't do,

>   now I did!
Pure, noble, free, like a cypress,

>   like a lily,
is how I suddenly am. I said,

>   *Oh no!*
Help me!

>   And that *Oh no!* became a rope
let down in my well. I've climbed out to stand here
in the sun. One moment I was at the bottom
of a dank, fearful narrowness, and the next,

I am not contained by this universe.

If every tip of every hair on me could speak,
I still couldn't say my gratitude.

In the middle of these streets and gardens, I stand and say
and say again, and it's all I say,
I wish everyone
could know what I know.'

Moses and the Shepherd

Moses heard a shepherd on the road praying,
> 'God,
where are you? I want to help you, to fix your shoes
and comb your hair. I want to wash your clothes
and pick the lice off. I want to bring you milk
to kiss your little hands and feet when it's time
for you to go to bed. I want to sweep your room
and keep it neat. God, my sheep and goats
are yours. All I can say, remembering you,
is *ayyyy* and *ahhhhhhhhh*.'
> Moses could stand it no longer.
'Who are you talking to?'
> 'The one who made us,
and made the earth and made the sky.'
> 'Don't talk about shoes
and socks with God! And what's this with *your little hands
and feet*? Such blasphemous familiarity sounds like
you're chatting with your uncles.
> Only something that grows
needs milk. Only someone with feet needs shoes. Not God!
Even if you meant God's human representatives,
as when God said, "I was sick, and you did not visit me,"
even then this tone would be foolish and irreverent.

Use appropriate terms. *Fatima* is a fine name
for a woman, but if you call a man *Fatima*,
it's an insult. Body-and-birth language
are right for us on this side of the river,
but not for addressing the origin,
> not for Allah.'

The shepherd repented and tore his clothes and sighed
and wandered out into the desert.

A sudden revelation

came then to Moses. God's voice:

You have separated me

from one of my own. Did you come as a Prophet to unite,
or to sever?

I have given each being a separate and unique way
of seeing and knowing and saying that knowledge.

What seems wrong to you is right for him.
What is poison to one is honey to someone else.

Purity and impurity, sloth and diligence in worship,
these mean nothing to me.

I am apart from all that.

Ways of worshipping are not to be ranked as better
or worse than one another.

Hindus do Hindu things.

The Dravidian Muslims in India do what they do.
It's all praise, and it's all right.

It's not me that's glorified in acts of worship.
It's the worshippers! I don't hear the words
they say. I look inside at the humility.

That broken-open lowliness is the reality,
not the language! Forget phraseology.
I want burning, burning.

Be friends

with your burning. Burn up your thinking
and your forms of expression!

Moses,

those who pay attention to ways of behaving
and speaking are one sort.

                    Lovers who burn
are another.
            Don't impose a property tax
on a burned-out village. Don't scold the Lover.
The 'wrong' way he talks is better than a hundred
'right' ways of others.
                    Inside the Kaaba
it doesn't matter which direction you point
your prayer rug!
                The ocean diver doesn't need snowshoes!
The love-religion has no code or doctrine,
                                    Only God.
So the ruby has nothing engraved on it!
It doesn't need markings.
                    God began speaking
deeper mysteries to Moses. Vision and words,
which cannot be recorded here, poured into
and through him. He left himself and came back.
He went to eternity and came back here.
Many times this happened.
                    It's foolish of me
to try and say this. If I did say it,
it would uproot our human intelligences.
It would shatter all writing pens.

Moses ran after the shepherd.
He followed the bewildered footprints,
in one place moving straight like a castle
across a chessboard. In another, sideways,
like a bishop.
            Now surging like a wave cresting,
now sliding down like a fish,
                        with always his feet
making geomancy symbols in the sand,
                                recording
his wandering state.

Moses finally caught up
with him.

'I was wrong. God has revealed to me
that there are no rules for worship.

Say whatever
and however your loving tells you to. Your sweet blasphemy
is the truest devotion. Through you a whole world
is freed.

Loosen your tongue and don't worry what comes out.
It's all the light of the spirit.'

The shepherd replied,
'Moses, Moses,

I've gone beyond even that.
You applied the whip and my horse shied and jumped
out of itself. The divine nature and my human nature
came together.

Bless your scolding hand and your arm.
I can't say what has happened.

What I'm saying now
is not my real condition. It can't be said.'

The shepherd grew quiet.

When you look in a mirror,
you see yourself, not the state of the mirror.
The flute player puts breath into a flute,
and who makes the music? Not the flute.
The flute player!

Whenever you speak praise
or thanksgiving to God, it's always like
this dear shepherd's simplicity.

When you eventually see
through the veils to how things really are,
you will keep saying again
and again,

'This is certainly not like
we thought it was!'

Joy at Sudden Disappointment

Whatever comes, comes from a need,
a sore distress, a hurting want.

Mary's pain made the baby Jesus.
Her womb opened its lips
and spoke the Word.

Every part of you has a secret language.
Your hands and your feet say what you've done.

And every need brings in what's needed.
Pain bears its cure like a child.

Having nothing produces provisions.
Ask a difficult question,
and the marvelous answer appears.

Build a ship, and there'll be water
to float it. The tender-throated
infant cries and milk drips
from the mother's breast.

Be thirsty for the ultimate water,
and then be ready for what will
come pouring from the spring.

A village woman once was walking by Muhammad.
She thought he was just an ordinary illiterate.
She didn't believe that he was a prophet.

She was carrying a two-month-old baby.
As she came near Muhammad, the baby turned
and said, 'Peace be with you, Messenger of God.'

The mother cried out, surprised and angry,
'What are you saying,
and how can you suddenly talk!'

The child replied, 'God taught me first,
and then Gabriel.'
                        'Who is this Gabriel?
I don't see anyone.'
                        'He is above your head,
Mother. Turn around. He has been telling me
many things.'
                        'Do you really see him?'
                                            'Yes.
He is continually delivering me from this
degraded state into sublimity.'

Muhammad then asked the child,
'What is your name?'

'Abdul Aziz, the servant of God, but this family
thinks I am concerned with world-energies.
I am as free of that as the truth of your prophecy is.'

So the little one spoke, and the mother
took in a fragrance that let her surrender
to that state.
                        When God gives this knowing,
inanimate stones, plants, animals, everything,
fills with unfolding significance.

The fish and the birds become protectors.
Remember the incident of Muhammad and the eagle.

It happened that as he was listening
to this inspired baby, he heard a voice
calling him to prayer. He asked for water

to perform ablutions. He washed his hands
and feet, and just as he reached for his boot,

an eagle snatched it away! The boot turned upsidedown
as it lifted, and a poisonous snake dropped out.

The eagle circled and brought the boot back,
saying, 'My helpless reverence for you
made this necessary. Anyone who acts
this presumptuously for a legalistic reason
should be punished!'
                    Muhammad thanked the eagle,
and said, 'What I thought was rudeness
was really love. You took away my grief,
and I was grieved! God has shown me everything
but at that moment I was preoccupied within myself.'
The eagle,
            'But chosen one, any clarity I have
comes from you!'
                    This spreading radiance
of a True Human Being has great importance.

Look carefully around you and recognize
the luminosity of souls. Sit beside those
who draw you to that.
                    Learn from this eagle story
that when misfortune comes, you must quickly praise.

Others may be saying, *Oh no*, but you
will be opening out like a rose
losing itself petal by petal.

Someone once asked a great sheikh
what sufism was.
                'The feeling of joy
when sudden disappointment comes.'

The eagle carries off Muhammad's boot
and saves him from snakebite.

Don't grieve for what doesn't come.
Some things that don't happen
keep disasters from happening.

* * * *

If the beloved is everywhere,
the lover is a veil,

but when living itself becomes
the Friend, lovers disappear.

* * * *

Story Water

A story is like water
that you heat for your bath.

It takes messages between the fire
and your skin. It lets them meet,
and it cleans you!

Very few can sit down
in the middle of the fire itself
like a salamander or Abraham.
We need intermediaries.

A feeling of fullness comes,
but usually it takes some bread
to bring it.

Beauty surrounds us,
but usually we need to be walking
in a garden to know it.

The body itself is a screen
to shield and partially reveal
the light that's blazing
inside your presence.

Water, stories, the body,
all the things we do, are mediums
that hide and show what's hidden.

Study them,
and enjoy this being washed
with a secret we sometimes know,
and then not.

8. Rough Metaphors:

More Teaching Stories

ON ROUGHNESS

Some of Rumi's metaphors are rough, and unacceptable to refined tastes. When Reynold Nicholson translated the *Mathnawi* into English in the 1920s, he chose to render some passages into Latin, supposing that anyone who knew enough Latin to read them would be properly shielded from taint. Rumi uses anything human beings do, no matter how scandalous or cruel or silly, as a lens to examine soul growth. A gourd crafted to serve as a flange, allowing a donkey's penis to enter a woman's vagina just to the point of her pleasure but not far enough to harm her, becomes a metaphor for a device a sheikh might use to put limits on a disciple. After another graphic, outrageously elaborated comparison of breadmaking with lovemaking, he concludes, 'Remember. The way you make love is the way God will be with you.' For Rumi, the bread of every experience offers nourishment.

Rough Metaphors

Someone said, 'there is no dervish, or if there is a dervish,
   that dervish is not there.'

Look at a candle flame in bright noon sunlight.
   If you put cotton next to it, the cotton will burn,
      but its light has become completely mixed
         with the sun.

That candlelight you can't find   is what's left of a dervish.

If you sprinkle one ounce of vinegar over
      two hundred tons of sugar,
            no one will ever taste the vinegar.

A deer faints in the paws of a lion. The deer becomes
      another glazed expression on the face of the lion.

These are rough metaphors for what happens to the lover.

There's no one more openly irreverent than a lover. He, or she,
   jumps up on the scale opposite eternity
         and claims to balance it.

And no one more secretly reverent.

A grammar lesson: 'The lover died.'
   'Lover' is subject and agent, but that can't be!
         The 'lover' is defunct.

Only grammatically is the dervish-lover a doer.

In reality, with he or she so overcome,
   so dissolved into love,
         all qualities of doingness
               disappear.

Birdwings

Your grief for what you've lost lifts a mirror
up to where you're bravely working.

Expecting the worst, you look, and instead,
here's the joyful face you've been wanting to see.

Your hand opens and closes and opens and closes.
If it were always a fist or always stretched open,
you would be paralyzed.

Your deepest presence is in every small contracting
                                        and expanding,
the two as beautifully balanced and coordinated
as birdwings.

I Come Before Dawn

Muhammad says,
                'I come before dawn
to chain you and drag you off.'
It's amazing, and funny, that you have to be pulled away
from being tortured, pulled out
into this Spring garden,
                        but that's the way it is.

Almost everyone must be bound and dragged here.
Only a few come on their own.

Children have to be made to go to school at first.
Then some of them begin to like it.
                        They run to school.
They expand with the learning.
                        Later, they receive money
because of something they've learned at school,
and they get really excited. They stay up all night,
as watchful and alive as thieves!

Remember the rewards you get for being obedient!

There are two types on the path. Those who come
against their will, the blindly religious people, and those
who obey out of love. The former have ulterior motives.
They want the midwife near, because she gives them milk.
The others love the beauty of the nurse.

The former memorize the prooftexts of conformity,
and repeat them. The latter disappear
into whatever draws them to God.

Both are drawn from the source.
Any moving's from the mover.
Any love from the beloved.

Checkmate

Borrow the beloved's eyes.
Look through them and you'll see the beloved's face
everywhere. No tiredness, no jaded boredom.
'I shall be your eye and your hand and your loving.'
Let that happen, and things
you have hated will become helpers.

A certain preacher always prays long and with enthusiasm
for thieves and muggers that attack people
on the street. 'Let your mercy, O Lord,
cover their insolence.'
He doesn't pray for the good,
but only for the blatantly cruel.
Why is this? his congregation asks.

'Because they have done me such generous favors.
Every time I turn back toward the things they want.
I run into them, they beat me, and leave me nearly dead
in the road, and I understand, again, that what they want
is not what I want. They keep me on the spiritual path.
That's why I honor them and pray for them.'

Those that make you return, for whatever reason,
to God's solitude, be grateful to them.
Worry about the others, who give you
delicious comforts that keep you from prayer.
Friends are enemies sometimes,
and enemies friends.

There is an animal called an *ushghur*, a porcupine.
If you hit it with a stick, it extends its quills
and gets bigger. The soul is a porcupine,
made strong by stick-beating.

So a prophet's soul is especially afflicted,
because it has to become so powerful.

A hide is soaked in tanning liquor and becomes leather.
If the tanner did not rub in the acid,
the hide would get foul-smelling and rotten.

The soul is a newly skinned hide, bloody and gross.
Work on it with manual discipline,
and the bitter tanning acid of grief,
and you'll become lovely, and *very* strong.

If you can't do this work yourself, don't worry.
You don't even have to make a decision,
one way or another. The Friend, who knows
a lot more than you do, will bring difficulties,
and grief, and sickness,

as medicine, as happiness,
as the essence of the moment when you're beaten,
when you hear *Checkmate*, and can finally say,
with Hallaj's voice,

I trust you to kill me.

An Awkward Comparison

This physical world has no two things alike.
Every comparison is awkwardly rough.

You can put a lion next to a man,
but the placing is hazardous to both.

Say the body is like this lamp.
It has to have a wick and oil. Sleep and food.
If it doesn't get those, it will die,
and it's always burning those up, trying to die.

But where is the sun in this comparison?
It rises, and the lamp's light
mixes with the day.
                    Oneness,
which is the reality, cannot be understood
with lamp and sun images. The blurring
of a plural into a unity is wrong.

No image can describe
what of our fathers and mothers,
our grandfathers and grandmothers, remains.

Language does not touch the one
who lives in each of us.

Two Kinds of Intelligence

There are two kinds of intelligence: one acquired,
as a child in school memorizes facts and concepts
from books and from what the teacher says,
collecting information from the traditional sciences
as well as from the new sciences.

With such intelligence you rise in the world.
You get ranked ahead or behind others
in regard to your competence in retaining
information. You stroll with this intelligence
in and out of fields of knowledge, getting always more
marks on your preserving tablets.

There is another kind of tablet, one
already completed and preserved inside you.
A spring overflowing its springbox. A freshness
in the center of the chest. This other intelligence
does not turn yellow or stagnate. It's fluid,
and it doesn't move from outside to inside
through the conduits of plumbing-learning.

This second knowing is a fountainhead
from within you, moving out.

Two Ways of Running

A certain man had a jealous wife
and a very, very appealing maidservant.

The wife was careful not to leave them alone,

ever. For six years they were never left
in a room together.
                    But then one day
at the public bath the wife suddenly remembered
that she'd left her silver washbasin at home.

'Please, go get the basin,' she told her maid.

The girl jumped to the task, because she knew
that she would finally get to be alone
with the master. She ran joyfully.
                              She flew,
and desire took them both so quickly
that they didn't even latch the door.

With great speed they joined each other.
When bodies blend in copulation,
spirits also merge.

Meanwhile, the wife back at the bathhouse,
washing her hair, 'What have I done!
I've set the cotton-wool on fire!
I've put the ram in with the ewe!'

She washed the clay soap off her hair and ran,
fixing her chador about her as she went.

The maid ran for love. The wife ran out of fear
and jealousy. There is a great difference.

The mystic flies moment to moment.
The fearful ascetic drags along month to month.

But also the length of a 'day' to a lover
may be fifty thousand years!

You can't understand this with your mind.
You must burst open!

Fear is nothing to a lover, a tiny piece of thread.
Love is a quality of God. Fear is an attribute
of those who think they serve God, but who are actually
preoccupied with penis and vagina.

You have read in the text where *They love him*
blends with *He loves them*.

Those joining loves
are both qualities of God. Fear is not.

What characteristics do God and human beings
have in common? What is the connection between
what lives in time and what lives in eternity?

If I kept talking about love,
a hundred new combinings would happen,
and still I would not say the mystery.

The fearful ascetic runs on foot, along the surface.
Lovers move like lightning and wind.

No contest.
Theologians mumble, rumble-dumble,
necessity and free will,
while lover and beloved

pull themselves
into each other.

The worried wife reaches the door
and opens it.

The maid, disheveled, confused, flushed,
unable to speak.

The husband begins his five-times prayer.

The wife enters this agitated scene.
As though experimenting with clothes,
the husband holds up some flaps and edges.

She sees his testicles and penis so wet, semen
still dribbling out, spurts of jism and vaginal juices
drenching the thighs of the maid.

                          The wife slaps him
on the side of the head,
                        'Is this the way
a man prays, with his balls?
                        Does your penis
long for union like this?
                        Is that why
her legs are so covered with this stuff?'

These are good questions
she's asking her 'ascetic' husband!

People who renounce desires
often turn, suddenly,
into hypocrites!

The Importance of Gourdcrafting

There was a maidservant
who had cleverly trained a donkey
to perform the services of a man.

From a gourd,
she had carved a flanged device
to fit on the donkey's penis,
to keep him from going too far into her.

She had fashioned it just to the point
of her pleasure, and she greatly enjoyed
the arrangement, as often as she could!

She thrived, but the donkey was getting
a little thin and tired looking.

The mistress began to investigate. One day
she peeked through a crack in the door
and saw the animal's marvelous member
and the delight of the girl
stretched under the donkey.

She said nothing. Later, she knocked on the door
and called the maid out on an errand,
a long and complicated errand.
I won't go into details.

The servant knew what was happening, though.
'Ah, my mistress,' she thought to herself,
'you should not send away the expert.

When you begin to work without full knowledge,
you risk your life. Your shame keeps you
from asking me about the gourd, but you must
have that to join with this donkey.
There's a trick you don't know!'

But the woman was too fascinated with her idea
to consider any danger. She led the donkey in
and closed the door, thinking, 'With no one around
I can shout in my pleasure.'
                                        She was dizzy
with anticipation, her vagina glowing
and singing like a nightingale.

She arranged the chair under the donkey,
as she had seen the girl do. She raised her legs
and pulled him into her.

                     Her fire kindled more,
and the donkey politely pushed as she urged him to,
pushed through and into her intestines,
and, without a word, she died.

The chair fell one way,
and she the other.

The room was smeared with blood.

                     Reader,
have you ever seen anyone martyred
for a donkey? Remember what the Qur'an
says about the torment of disgracing yourself.

Don't sacrifice your life to your animal-soul!

If you die of what that leads you to do,
you are just like this woman on the floor.
She is an image of immoderation.

Remember her,
and keep your balance.

The maidservant returns and says, 'Yes, you saw
my pleasure, but you didn't see the gourd
that put a limit on it. You opened
your shop before a master
taught you the craft.'

Breadmaking

There was a feast. The king
was heartily in his cups.

He saw a learned scholar walking by.
'Bring him in and give him
some of this fine wine.'

Servants rushed out and brought the man
to the king's table, but he was not
receptive. 'I had rather drink poison!
I have never tasted wine and never will!
Take it away from me!'

He kept on with these loud refusals,
disturbing the atmosphere of the feast.

This is how it sometimes is
at God's table.

Someone who has *heard* about ecstatic love,
but never tasted it, disrupts the banquet.

If there were a secret passage
from his ear to his throat, everything
in him would change. Initiation would occur.

As it is, he's all fire and no light,
all husk and no kernel.

The king gave orders. 'Cupbearer,
do what you must!'

This is how your invisible guide acts,
the chess champion across from you
that always wins. He cuffed
the scholar's head and said,
                              'Taste!'
And, 'Again!'
                The cup was drained
and the intellectual started singing
and telling ridiculous jokes.

He joined the garden, snapping his fingers
and swaying. Soon, of course,
he had to pee.

He went out, and there, near the latrine,
was a beautiful woman, one of the king's harem.

His mouth hung open. He wanted her!
Right then, he wanted her!
And she was not unwilling.

They fell to, on the ground.
You've seen a baker rolling dough.
He kneads it gently at first,
then more roughly.

He pounds it on the board.
It softly groans under his palms.
Now he spreads it out
and rolls it flat.

Then he bunches it,
and rolls it all the way out again,
thin. Now he adds water,
and mixes it well.

Now salt,
and a little more salt.

Now he shapes it delicately
to its final shape
and slides it into the oven,
which is already hot.

You remember breadmaking!
This is how your desire
tangles with a desired one.

And it's not just a metaphor
for a man and a woman making love.

Warriors in battle do this too.
A great mutual embrace is always happening
between the eternal and what dies,
between essence and accident.

The sport has different rules
in every case, but it's basically
the same, and remember:

the way you make love is the way
God will be with you.

So these two were lost in their sexual trance.
They did not care anymore about feasting
or wine. Their eyes were closed like
perfectly matching calligraphy lines.

The king went looking for the scholar,
and when he saw them there coupled, commented,

'Well, as it is said, "A good king
must serve his subjects from his own table!"'

There is joy, a winelike freedom
that dissolves the mind and restores
the spirit, and there is manly fortitude
like the king's, a reasonableness
that accepts the bewildered lostness.

But meditate now on steadfastness
and clarity, and let those be the wings
that lift and soar through the celestial spheres.

9. Solomon Poems:

The Far Mosque

ON SOLOMON

Solomon and Sheba are types for the courtship story going on in all of Rumi's poetry. King Solomon (luminous divine wisdom) sends messengers to coax the Queen of Sheba (the bodily soul) to leave her kingdom and come live with him. She coyly sends envoys back with foolishly inappropriate gifts, and when she herself finally arrives, she does so with the one thing she cannot bear to leave, her filigreed throne (the body). The marriage of spiritual vision with the body finds many metaphors throughout Rumi's art: Jesus riding the lean donkey, the way a river dissolves into the ocean, dawn sunlight filling a ruby, the nightsky contained in a person's eyes. The ecstatic astonishment within Rumi's poetry comes from his firsthand wonder at how the ocean comes to court the drop!

I once had a dream where I was supposed to give a lecture on Rumi and D. H. Lawrence, but I couldn't find the lecture hall. The challenge was to connect Lawrence's dark body-knowledge with Rumi's spiritual enlightenment. I ended up in some anteroom eating hors d'oeuvres. The mind knows when it's been assigned work outside its purview. Rumi's poetry nourishes the part of us that wants a continually unfolding truth, not some confined conclusion. The relationship of soul wisdom and the body, Solomon and Sheba, is a dynamic dance that keeps generating stories.

Sheba's Gifts to Solomon

Queen Sheba loads forty mules with gold bricks
as gifts for Solomon. When her envoy and his party
reach the wide plain leading to Solomon's palace,
they see that the top layer of the entire plain
is pure gold. They travel on gold
for forty days!
                    What foolishness to take gold
to Solomon, when the *dirt* of his land
is gold. You who think to offer
your intelligence, reconsider. The mind
is less than road dust.

The embarrassing commonness they bring only
slows them down. They argue. They discuss
turning back, but they continue,
carrying out the orders of their queen.

Solomon laughs when he sees them unloading
gold bars.
          'When have I asked you
for a sop for my soup? I don't want gifts
from you. I want you to be ready
for the gifts I give.

You worship a planet that creates gold.
Worship instead the one who creates the universe.
You worship the sun. The sun is only a cook.
Think of a solar eclipse. What if you get attacked
at midnight? Who will help you then?'

These astronomical matters fade.
Another intimacy happens,

a sun at midnight,
with no east, no night or day.

The clearest intelligences faint,
seeing the solar system flickering,
so tiny in that immense lightness.

Drops fall into a vapor, and the vapor explodes
into a galaxy. Half a ray strikes a patch of darkness.
A new sun appears.
                        One slight, alchemical gesture,
and saturnine qualities form inside
the planet Saturn.

The sensuous eye needs sunlight to see.
Use another eye.
                        Vision is luminous.
Sight is igneous, and sun-fire light very dark.

Solomon to Sheba

Solomon says to the messengers from Sheba,
'I send you back as messengers to her.

Tell her this refusal of her gift
of gold is better than acceptance,

because with it she can learn what *we* value.
She loves her throne, but actually it keeps

her from passing through the doorway
that leads to a true majesty.

Tell her, one surrendering bow is sweeter
than a hundred empires, is itself a kingdom.

Be dizzy and wandering like Ibrahim,
who suddenly left everything.

In a narrow well things look backward
from how they are. Stones and metal objects

seem treasure, as broken pottery does
to children pretending to buy and sell.

Tell her, Joseph sat in such a well,
then reached to take the rope that rose

to a new understanding. The *alchemy*
of a changing life is the only truth.'

Sheba's Hesitation

Lovers of God, sometimes a door opens,
and a human being becomes a way
for grace to come through.

I see various herbs in the kitchen garden,
each with its own bed, garlic, capers, saffron,
and basil, each watered differently to help it mature.

We keep the delicate ones separate from the turnips,
but there's room for all in this unseen world, so vast
that the Arabian desert gets lost in it like a single hair

in the ocean. Imagine that you are Sheba
trying to decide whether to go to Solomon!
You're haggling about how much to pay

for shoeing a donkey, when you could be seated
with one who is always in union with God,
who carries a beautiful garden inside himself.

You could be moving in a circuit without wing,
nourished without eating, sovereign without a throne.
No longer subject to fortune, you could be *luck* itself,

if you would rise from sleep, leave
the market arguing, and learn that
your own essence *is* your wealth.

Sheba's Throne

When the Queen of Sheba came to Solomon,
she left behind her kingdom and her wealth
the same way lovers leave their reputations.

Her servants meant nothing to her,
less than a rotten onion.

Her palaces and orchards,
so many piles of dung.

She heard the inner meaning of *LA!* No!
She came to Solomon with nothing, except
her throne! As the writer's pen becomes

a friend, as the tool the workman uses
day after day becomes deeply familiar, so
her filigreed throne was her one attachment.

I would explain more about this phenomenon,
but it would take too long.

It was a large throne and difficult to transport,
because it couldn't be taken apart, being as
cunningly put together as the human body.

Solomon saw that her heart was open to him
and that this throne would soon be repulsive
to her. 'Let her bring it,' he said. 'It will

become a lesson to her like the old shoes
and jacket are to Ayaz. She can look at
that throne and see how far she's come.'

In the same way, God keeps the process
of generation constantly before us:

the smooth skin and the semen
and the growing embryo.

When you see a pearl on the bottom,
you reach through the foam and broken sticks
on the surface. When the sun comes up, you forget
about locating the constellation of Scorpio.

When you see the splendor of union,
the attractions of duality seem poignant
and lovely, but much less interesting.

Solomon's Crooked Crown

Solomon was busy judging others,
when it was his personal thoughts
that were disrupting the community.

His crown slid crooked on his head.
He put it straight, but the crown went
awry again. Eight times this happened.

Finally he began to talk to his headpiece.
'Why do you keep tilting over my eyes?'

'I have to. When your power loses compassion,
I have to show what such a condition looks like.'

Immediately Solomon recognized the truth.
He knelt and asked forgiveness.
The crown centered itself on his crown.

When something goes wrong, accuse yourself first.
Even the wisdom of Plato or Solomon
can wobble and go blind.

Listen when your crown reminds you
of what makes you cold toward others,
as you pamper the greedy energy inside.

The Far Mosque

The place that Solomon made to worship in,
called the Far Mosque, is not built of earth
and water and stone, but of intention and wisdom
and mystical conversation and compassionate action.

Every part of it is intelligence and responsive
to every other. The carpet bows to the broom.
The door knocker and the door swing together
like musicians. This heart sanctuary *does*
exist, but it can't be described. Why try!

Solomon goes there every morning and gives guidance
with words, with musical harmonies, and in actions,
which are the deepest teaching. A prince is just
a conceit until he *does* something with generosity.

*   *   *   *

A bird delegation came to Solomon complaining,
'Why is it you never criticize the nightingale?'

'Because my way,' the nightingale explained
for Solomon, 'is different. Mid-March
to mid-June I sing. The other

nine months, while you
continue chirping,
I'm silent.'

Notes

On Rumi

Fariddin Attar (1119–1230) was the great perfumist and physician–poet, author of *The Conference of the Birds*. He is said to have met Rumi in Damascus when Rumi was a boy of twelve traveling with his father. Attar immediately recognized Rumi's spiritual eminence. He saw the father walking ahead of the son and said, 'Here comes a sea followed by an ocean.' He gave the boy his *Asranama*, a book about the entanglement of the soul in the material world.

Annemarie Schimmel has been immersed in Rumi for over forty years. Her scholarship and devotion are magnificent. *The Triumphal Sun: A Study of the Works of Jalaloddin Rumi* (1978) and *I Am Wind, You Are Fire: The Life and Work of Rumi* (1992) are classics in the field.

A Note on the Organization

Alast is the primordial covenant that occurs when God addresses the not-yet-created humanity, 'Am I not your lord? *Alastu bi-rabbikum*.' Rumi hears the question as a creative music that makes all creatures come forth in a loving dance of reply, 'Yes!'

1. The Pickaxe

'*Zikr*': Zikr (or *dhikr*) means remembrance. In a practical sense it refers to the internal or external repetition of the phrase *La'illaha il'Allahu* ('there is no reality but God; there is only God'). The *zikr* is said to have at least three parts. The first part, *La'illaha*, is the denial, the abandonment of everything, the depths. The second part, *il'Allah*, is the actual intrusion, the explosion into the individual, of divine presence. *Hu*, the third part, is the out-breathing of that divine presence.

One sufi teacher, Bawa Muhaiyaddeen, advised his students to repeat and reflect upon the *zikr* with every breath. A student asked the teacher, 'But how is that possible? I mean, how could anyone *do* that?' The teacher said, 'It is like driving a car. At first you think it is difficult, but you get used to it. It becomes natural. After awhile, you can even drive and talk at the same time.'

2. Art as Flirtation with Surrender

'Omar and the Old Poet': Omar (d. 644) was the second caliph, designated as such by Abu Bakr on his deathbed. Omar is famous for his strong will and his direct, impetuous character. He formed the Islamic state and expanded it into Syria, Iraq, Egypt, and Libya.

3. Union

'Ayaz and the King's Pearl': Ayaz is the servant who is completely obedient to his master, King Mahmud (which means 'Praise to the end!'). This love between king and slave as an image of that between lover and beloved is a story retold in many mystical sources (Ghazzali, Attar, Sanai). Rumi's version adds a striking new touch. Ayaz goes to a secret closet every morning. The courtiers suspect he's hiding something, but the 'treasure' turns out to be only an old sheepskin jacket and Ayaz's worn-out work shoes. He goes there to meditate on them as reminders of his state before he was called to the king's service. Rumi says that to remember who one was before the advent of grace is to know one's lord.

6. The Howling Necessity

'Love Dogs': *Khidr* means, literally, 'the green one.' Khidr is known throughout the Islamic world. He exists on the edge between the seen and the unseen. When Moses vows to find the place 'where the two seas meet,' meaning where the spiritual and the worldly mix, he meets Khidr. Although not mentioned by name in the Qur'an, Khidr is associated with the person described as 'one of our servants whom We [God] had given mercy from Us, and We had taught him knowledge proceeding from Us' (Qur'an 18:64, Arberry translation).

In this passage, Moses wants to follow Khidr and learn from him, but Khidr says, 'If you follow me, you must not question anything I do. You must be patient and wait for my explanations.' Moses agrees, but as Khidr performs apparent outrages (sinking a boat, killing a boy), Moses cannot restrain his alarm, and Khidr leaves him after explaining the hidden reasons for his actions. Khidr represents the inner dimension, which transcends form. He is the personification of the revealing function of the metaphysical intellect, the 'prophetic soul.' He especially appears to solitaries, those who are cut off from normal channels of spiritual instruction. The sufi mystic Ibrahim, who gave up his external kingdom for the kingdom within, said this of Khidr: 'I lived four years in the wilderness. Khidr the Green Ancient was my companion. He taught me the Great Name of God.'

Khidr is connected philologically with Elijah and with Utnapishtim of the Gilgamesh epic. He may be a partial source, along with Druidic lore, for the enigmatic Green Knight in the Middle English poem 'Sir Gawain and the Green Knight.'

References

The numbers for the quatrains and the odes (# followed by a number) refer to
the numbering in Furuzanfar's edition of *Kulliyat-e Shams*, 8 vols. (Teheran:
Amir Kabir Press, 1957–1966). The *Mathnawi* references (a roman numeral,
I–VI, followed by line numbers) are to Reynold Nicholson's edition (London:
Luzac, 1925–1940). The page references to Arberry are to A. J. Arberry's
translation, *The Rubaiyat of Jalal al-din Rumi* (London: Emery Walker, 1949).

1. The Pickaxe

'Who Makes These Changes?' VI, 3682–87; 'Why Wine Is Forbidden,' IV,
2154–58; 'On Resurrection Day,' V, 2211–20; 'The Dream That Must Be
Interpreted,' IV, 3654–67, 3628–52; 'The Pickaxe,' IV, 2540–59; '*Zikr*,' IV,
435–66; 'The Core of Masculinity,' VI, 1430–45; 'I honor those who try . . . ,'
#828; 'Dervish at the Door,' VI, 1250–67.

2. Art as Flirtation with Surrender

'Omar and the Old Poet,' I, 2076, 2086–2101, 2106–9, 2163–66, 2175–2220;
'An Egypt That Doesn't Exist,' #1754; 'Chinese Art and Greek Art,' I, 3462–85,
3499; 'In your light I learn . . . ,' Arberry, 178a; 'Drumsound rises on the air . . . ,'
Arberry, 64a; 'Are you jealous of the ocean's generosity? . . . ,' Arberry, 7b.

3. Union

'Gnats Inside the Wind,' III, 4624–33, 4644–59; 'Meadowsounds,' #3079;
'Ayaz and the King's Pearl,' V, 4035–64, 4075–79, 4083–4117, 4189–92,
4195–4215; 'Put This Design in Your Carpet,' V, 3292–99, 3310–24; 'Hallaj,'
#1288; 'We Three,' #2395; 'I am filled with you . . . ,' #168.

4. The Sheikh

'Chickpea to Cook,' III, 4160–68, 4197–4208; 'I Have Such a Teacher,' #2015; 'Sublime Generosity,' #1373; 'Like This,' #1826; 'A Bowl,' #2805; 'Wax,' #1628; 'No Room for Form,' #1145; 'Childhood Friends,' I, 3150–75, 3192–3227; 'The Mouse and the Camel,' II, 3436–74; 'These gifts from the Friend . . . ,' #33; 'The Lame Goat,' III, 1114–27.

5. Recognizing Elegance

'Father Reason,' IV, 3259–70; 'A craftsman pulled a reed . . . ,' #612; 'Humble living does not diminish . . . ,' #397; 'New Moon, Hilal,' VI, 1111–1215; 'Body Intelligence,' IV, 3678–3703, 3708–10; 'The Seed Market,' IV, 2611–25.

6. The Howling Necessity

'Love Dogs,' III, 189–211; 'Cry Out in Your Weakness,' II, 1932–60; 'The Debtor Sheikh,' II, 376–444. 'You that come to birth . . . ,' Arberry, 189b.

7. Teaching Stories

'Nasuh,' V, 2228–2316; 'Moses and the Shepherd,' II, 1720–96; 'Joy at Sudden Disappointment,' III, 3204–65; 'If the beloved is everywhere . . . ,' I, 30; 'Story Water,' V, 228–36.

8. Rough Metaphors

'Rough Metaphors,' III, 3669–85; 'Birdwings,' III, 3762–66; 'I Come Before Dawn,' III, 4587–4600; 'Checkmate,' IV, 74–109; 'An Awkward Comparison,' IV, 419–33; 'Two Kinds of Intelligence,' IV, 1960–68; 'Two Ways of Running,' V, 2163–2204, 2210; 'The Importance of Gourdcrafting,' V, 1333–1405; 'Breadmaking,' VI, 3914–79.

9. *Solomon Poems*

'Sheba's Gifts to Solomon,' IV, 563–97; 'Solomon to Sheba,' IV, 653–77; 'Sheba's Hesitation,' IV, 1082–1113; 'Sheba's Throne,' IV, 863–89; 'Solomon's Crooked Crown,' IV, 1901–7, 1913, 1918–19, 1923; 'The Far Mosque,' IV, 475–86; 'A bird delegation came to Solomon . . . ,' Arberry, 12b.

Index of Titles

Index of First Lines

PENGUIN

ARKANA

NEW AGE BOOKS FOR MIND, BODY & SPIRIT

With over 200 titles currently in print, Arkana is the leading name in quality books for mind, body and spirit. Arkana encompasses the spirituality of both East and West, ancient and new. A vast range of interests is covered, including Psychology and Transformation, Health, Science and Mysticism, Women's Spirituality, Zen, Western Traditions and Astrology.

If you would like a catalogue of Arkana books, please write to:

Sales Department – Arkana
Penguin Books USA Inc.
375 Hudson Street
New York, NY 10014

Arkana Marketing Department
Penguin Books Ltd
27 Wrights Lane
London W8 5TZ

Available while stocks last.

PENGUIN

ARKANA

NEW AGE BOOKS FOR MIND, BODY & SPIRIT

BY THE SAME AUTHOR

Whoever Brought Me Here Will Have to Take Me Home
Translated by Coleman Barks

The poet Jami referred to Rumi's major works as 'the Koran in Persian', such was the significance and religious influence of his poetry and meditations.

Rumi was greatly influenced by a man called Shams, a wandering Dervish, with whom he developed a great spiritual rapport. This relationship inspired some of Rumi's finest work as a poet and mystic, in particular the Mathnawi, his great work whose focus moves from the everyday to the esoteric, from the severe to the sensuous.

Whoever Brought Me Here Will Have to Take Me Home is a selection of Rumi's ecstatic poetry whose brilliance, humour, humanity and ideology has been brought to contemporary English readers by the superb translation of Coleman Barks.